Vaughan Garrett's
FAVORITE
FINDS™

Vaughan Garrett's Favorite Finds

Library of Congress Cataloging-in-Publication Data

Garrett, Vaughan L.
  Vaughan Garrett's Favorite Finds: A decade of amazing recoveries made by Garrett Metal Detectors customers / Vaughan L. Garrett.
      p. cm.
  Includes bibliographical references.
  ISBN 978-0-9835451-1-8 (alk. paper)
  1. Treasure troves. 2. Metal detectors. I. Title.

Library of Congress Control Number:
2018968131

Published by RAM Books
A Division of Garrett Metal Detectors
Edited by Stephen L. Moore

To order a RAM book, call 1-800-527-4011
or visit www.garrett.com for more information.

DEDICATED TO MY PARENTS
CHARLES AND ELEANOR GARRETT,
who provided the opportunity for
this compilation to be possible.

WE CELEBRATE YOUR GARRETT FINDS

Foreword by Stephen L. Moore

Charles and Eleanor Garrett founded Garrett Metal Detectors in 1964, with their original goal being that of building better metal detectors than what Charles had been able to purchase on the market for his own use.

Nearly 55 years later, Garrett Metal Detectors continues to produce the highest quality detectors with the latest technology, making them available at fair prices with the best possible customer service.

During his life, Charles Garrett spent countless hours in the field, testing each new product his company planned to introduce to the public. Once his company's inventions were released for treasure hunters to enjoy, the Garrett family was always thrilled to see what their customers discovered with their Garretts.

In his own decades of searching, Charles literally traveled the world, testing his detectors in all kinds of soil conditions during his quests for treasure. His travels took him to Civil War sites in Tennessee, Louisiana, and Virginia. He found treasure on every continent except Antarctica. Garrett hunted in Europe and even Egypt, traveling into dozens of countries in company with friends who shared in his searches for artifacts and coins that often predated the life of Jesus Christ.

Garrett ventured into Idaho, Oregon, Colorado, Canada, Australia, and even Mexico in search of precious metals like gold and silver. He visited historic sites in the Caribbean where former forts and battle sites bore evidence of the explorers of previous centuries.

The adjacent page contains just a few of Charles Garrett's personal favorite find items. The balance of *Favorite Finds* is dedicated to a few of the countless discoveries made every day by customers using Garrett's metal detectors. Most of these recoveries were made in the past decade and were submitted to Garrett as part of an online rewards contest titled Favorite Finds.

Charles Garrett passed away in 2015 at the age of 83, but his passion for treasure hunting will live for generations to come through the discoveries his customers will continue to make with detectors bearing his name. *Favorite Finds* is thus a celebration of the sport of metal detecting and the rich pleasure it brings to so many thousands of people to this day.

Vaughan Garrett has conducted, since 2009, a "Favorite Find of the Month" contest for the company's loyal users. Customers are encouraged to submit their own photos and stories of their best finds as often as they choose. From these submissions, Vaughan selects one or more winners each month for both the U.S. and international markets, and rewards them with a pinpointer, metal detector, or other Garrett-branded item.

Two sections of this book display a portion of the "Favorite Finds" winners Vaughan has selected over the years. It would take a book in itself to showcase each and every one of the winning finds. For now, the Garrett family hopes you enjoy this sampling of treasure finds . . . and encourages you to get out there and seek your own gold, silver, jewelry, and historic relics. Happy hunting!

Left: Eleanor Garrett and her son Vaughan enjoy seeing and hearing about some of the finds made by Dallas-area treasure hunters Bob and Nelda Forston.

Above: Charles Garrett and his son Vaughan, holding Greek and Roman coins they found on a detecting trip years earlier.

Charles Garrett holds up a gold British military insignia piece he recovered from a British fort site used in the late 1700s to defend the Caribbean island of Antigua against French troops. At right is a collection of military relics Garrett found on Antigua near the ruins of the military fort the British called Shirley Heights.

Garrett's most prized find was this 16th century Spanish icon of the Virgin Mary with Christ child. He found it with a *Master Hunter* on the Caribbean island of Guadeloupe.

Charles is seen here in 1988 in the Red Sea near Egypt with a prototype *Sea Hunter* detector, on a quest to find Biblical chariots.

Right: "Snow White" is a 7.656"-tall gem among the Charles Garrett collection. Found in Western Australia's Golden Mile, the 80-ounce rock was treated by chemist Virgil Hutton to remove the iron—leaving only the white quartz and embedded gold.

Left: Garrett with two caches of high grade silver pieces he discovered where a miner had hidden them near an abandoned commercial mine in Canada.

(Right) This case shows a sampling of the historic finds Michael Bennett has made while water hunting with his *AT Pro*.

U.S. FAVORITE FINDS

THOUGHTS ON MY U.S. FAVORITES

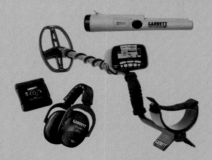

Vaughan Garrett

One of the highlights of every month during the past ten years has always been the time I spend reviewing all the incredible treasure finds our customers make with their Garrett brand metal detectors. Since 2009, I have selected hundreds of "Favorite Find of the Month" winners from the stories and photos our faithful fans send in to Garrett.

I've often selected multiple U.S. and international winners in the same month. My criteria has always been based on what excites ME the most, meaning that some winners were not the rarest or most valuable find that month. I might have been motivated by a great history lesson, a superb photograph, or perhaps some heart-felt emotion that came with their stories.

In this book's first section, I've selected a sampling of some of my Favorite Finds winners from the United States and included their photos and stories. Presented here are some of my favorite "Favorites."

Thank you to everyone who has submitted finds over the years. Keep it up, because you never know when we might put your picture in our newsletter or select you as a monthly winner!

Through the years, I've given away hundreds of metal detectors, pinpointers, and Z-Lynk wireless kits to my Favorite Finds winners.

Joseph P. of Connecticut was one of my early Favorite Finds winners in 2009. Using his *ACE 250*, Joseph found this Harrisburg and Waterbury Chamber of Commerce badge from 1926.

There were several factors that added up to Joseph being one of my winners:

Rarity   – only several hundred of these produced.
History   – designed for special political event.
Research   – determined political significance in 1926.
Condition – good photography reveals legibility and preservation of brass with no scars evident during recovery.
Search   – recovered in difficult search conditions in area with trash and brush.

I think any treasure hunter would be thrilled to find a gold coin, a gold nugget, or a gold ring. Well, how about a gold coin nugget ring?

A very fortunate Curtis M. of Massachusetts discovered his first gold coin while searching with his *GTI 2500* on a New Hampshire beach. It was a gorgeous St. Gaudens Walking Liberty coin in excellent condition. Even more exciting was the fact that the gold coin Curtis dug was mounted into a gold nugget ring!

 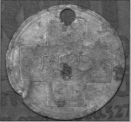

Raymond B. of Tennessee found this 1898 Spanish-American War dog tag at 10 inches with a *GTI 2500*. Raymond contacted the Spanish-American War History Board, who determined it belonged to Private Frank Blakemore (who was later a Second Lieutenant), and his great-grandson was notified. Raymond established contact with Blakemore to return the dog tag to where it belonged…with the family.

Brandon H. of Georgia found this Confederate States of America buckle with his *AT Pro*.

One of my 2012 Favorite Finds *(seen at lower right of this page)* was this impressive Masonic ring, found by Charles G. of Colorado with his *GTI 2500*. He was searching empty city lots when his detector gave out "a solid repeating signal that stayed right in between foil and nickel. Well, I dug it and out comes this 10k tri-colored gold Masonic ring with a diamond!" said Charles. "Needless to say, my pacemaker was put to the test that day! I took it to a local jeweler and he said it dated to the early 1900s, and appraised it at around $700 to $800 in its present dug condition, and with a little TLC from a jeweler the price would double."

The ring has special meaning for Charles. "My grandfather, his father, and his father were all Masons," he said. "I offered it to my friends as it was found on their property, and they said, 'No, it is yours. You found it.' Now, my new ring is with my grandfather's Masonic ring that he always had on. My grandmother gave it to me when he passed away. If he was still with us, I would have given it to him."

This 1848 pre-Civil War revolver was found by Jeremy P. of Montana with his *AT Pro*.

Sterling Elks watch fob, with the owner's name (E. T. Josey of Huntsville, Texas) engraved on it. It was found by Bob F. of Texas, using his *AT Pro*. Bob found that Josey was born in 1843, served in the Civil War, settled in Huntsville in 1870, and lived there until his death in 1925.

Above: John V. from New York found this 1810–1812 brass U.S. Navy button with his *AT Pro*.

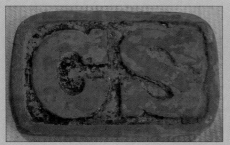

ACE 150 user Andy B. of Texas found this Confederate buckle while hunting near the Chickamauga battlefield.

Steven S. of Arkansas found this Boy Scout Good Luck coin—struck to commemorate the founding of the Boy Scouts of America in 1910—with his *ACE 350*. In his submission story, Steven stated, "Good luck follows you when you use Garrett."

Steven's find reminds me that my father, Charles Garrett, was a Boy Scout, and that he continued to support the organization. Being a Boy Scout taught my father much about land and survival and pride and laid the groundwork for a mind that helped shape Garrett Metal Detectors.

Virginia Military Institute gold gilded Civil War button, found by Jeffrey P. of Virginia with his *AT Pro*.

War of 1812 artillery belt plate, found with an *AT Pro* by Brian P. of New York.

William M. of Colorado found this large gold nugget 12" deep with his *AT Gold*.

Rose gold 23-diamond ring, found by *AT Max* user Ray H. of Oklahoma.

Civil War-era local Texas button for the Waco Guards company, found by Todd G. of Illinois with an *AT Pro*.

William F. from Connecticut found this six-coin cache during "a day I will never, ever forget." He gives credit to his digging buddies Kevin and Doug, who had invited him to hunt a 1770s homestead that had been converted into a bed and breakfast retreat.

Mark L. of Texas found a Purple Heart military medal with his *ACE 350*.

"Swinging my *AT Pro*," he said, "I hit an area near an old oak tree and got an iffy signal but on every other pass I would get a sweet high tone that was registering as high as 87 on the ID, so I dug. Three to four inches down I begin finding pottery and glass, then I hit an old iron nail, which explains the messy tone. Further digging, I see the rim of a silver coin…my excitement exploded. I called to Doug and he came running to video the dig.

"Upon pulling the coin and running water over it, we discovered it is a Spanish reale. We were both floored, and as any detectorist should do, I rechecked my hole and *bam!* ANOTHER Spanish Reale. Now, I think this is not happening to me on New Year's Day. At this point, the homestead owners come out because of the excitement and I recheck the hole. *BAM!* Another target. I literally had to sit down… my legs were jelly…and you guessed it another Spanish reale. Fast forward a few moments and more digging reveals one more reale and an 1819 Capped Bust Quarter!

"So, I figured what the heck? Let's scan the hole again and, you guessed it…another target, only this time it wasn't silver but a Capped Bust 5-dollar gold piece from 1812! At this point, I'm ready to run down the street screaming because I'm not this lucky EVER! And here I am, a year into metal detecting on January 1st digging what some people have tried to find for over 50 years. This is a day I will never, ever forget!"

Daniel C. from Alaska, shared a story of a discovery he made on a very cold day in 2013 with his *AT Gold*. "Our hunt took us into a new area, where I dug this military dog tag *(shown below)* at about 8 inches, with the name Floyd Haddenham on it. With some help and some research we found the twin brother, Lloyd Haddenham *(seen holding the recovered tag above)* in Ohio, who was able to confirm this was his brother's dog tag from his second enlistment when he volunteered for the Korean War. And now, this lost family heirloom will be passed down through the generations along with the rest of his military medals and ribbons."

This Civil War saddle ornament was found by Randall B. of Indiana, with his *ACE 350*, while hunting with a buddy near a local quarry.

1901 $10 gold coin, found by Ronny R. of Texas with an *AT Pro*.

David A. *(right)* of Oregon found this 14k gold ring with 35 diamonds with his *ACE 250*. A jeweler estimated its value at $15,000.

This British military buckle, worn by a member of the 53rd Regiment of Foot, was discovered by Dave H. from New Hampshire with his *ACE 350*. Per Dave, it dates to about 1775.

Kurt W. from Pennsylvania found this Washington centennial pin about six inches deep, while hunting near a row of pine trees with his *AT Pro*.

Justin H. of Indiana found this heavily engraved railroad pocket watch with his *AT Pro*. "It appears to be gold plated, but it could be a low karat gold," he said.

"I struck gold in California," said John W. of Texas. "On a trip to visit my ailing father, I was able to take a little time to do a little dirt fishing. I went to a park that I used to take my kids to nearly 30 years ago. After about an hour, the *AT Pro* sang out with a Target ID in the 60s. Four inches down, this beauty emerged. My first gold ring in three years of detecting."

John's 10k gold ring included 45 diamonds!

Right: David J. from California found this 1845 2.5-dollar gold coin with his *AT Pro*. He was searching a local beach that had been carved up by a storm.

Left: Michael F. from Tennessee made this great find while hunting a residential block that was being demolished near his home. Using his *ACE 250*, Michael found this World War II Sharpshooter's Medal and returned it to the nephew of a soldier who had earned it during the Battle of the Bulge.

Terry S. from Illinois found a gold ring with 14 diamonds while detecting a volleyball pit with his *AT Pro*. Terry said, "It was a solid 51 signal and was about 7 inches deep in the sand."

Stone K. of Alabama reports on this amazing discovery he made: "While detecting a very small permission from a house built in the 1920s, I made an incredible recovery! After digging a few Wheaties and whatever else, I got a silver quarter type signal. After popping my plug, I realized the target was deep and much larger than a quarter. It was an Alabama state seal sword plate! A very rare Confederate plate that I never could have anticipated. Turns out the ground I was hunting has some history. The *AT Pro* does it again! Woo-hooo!"

Avid Arkansas treasure hunter Bill F. found this Western Kentucky University class ring while detecting on a lake with his *AT Pro*. Working with a research team at the WKU Alumni Association, Bill was able to return the engraved 1964 ring to its owner, who had lost it while fishing at the lake 44 years earlier.

Cody D. from Vermont was "awestruck" when he dug this rare 1797 Vermont copper coin with his *AT Pro*. "I took it home to research the variety and found out it was the rare Ryder 15," said Cody. "Only 19 or 20 others are known to exist!"

This 1650s monogrammed IHS Jesuit trade ring was found by Brandon M. from New York with his *AT Pro*. He had been digging "tons of scrap copper" reading in the mid-50s on his Target ID, when he decided to dig this "semi-sketchy" signal. "When I saw the front, I nearly had a heart attack," said Brandon. "I dug it in a field that had long houses and captured Christians during the 1650s. I still can't believe it!"

Brian L. from Texas found this diamond and ruby ring while water hunting with his *AT Pro*. "I got a strong 42 signal and decided to go for it," he said. "I thought I was on the trail of another pull tab but when I pulled up the scoop and saw a shimmering gold band staring at me through the sand and gravel, all I could think was, 'Hello, beautiful!' The ring is hallmarked 14k and 585 inside the band. I tested all 16 diamonds and they tested real!"

Logan R. from Tennessee made these Civil War finds near a mid-1800s home with his *AT Pro*. "The owner told me that the place had been pounded by detectorists already but I was more than welcome to look around," said Logan. "I was pretty confident that with the right setup, I could maybe pick out a few small relics that may have been missed.

"I was starting to lose hope, but I came up on an odd squeaker tone. I was very surprised when an eagle cuff button popped out! I excitedly went back to digging. I checked the hole again with my *Pro-Pointer* and got a beep! Another cuff button! I did this for an entire hour, pulling buttons out left and right, some coat buttons and some cuffs. I wound up digging 20 eagle buttons out of this one spot!"

Paul M. from Louisiana recovered this ring while water hunting with his *AT Gold*. He said he was "waist deep when I got a solid tone that was 45 no matter what direction you checked it. One scoop down and out it popped: 6.3 grams of 14k white gold, one pear-cut center diamond that is .4 cts, and a total of 59 diamond chips for a total weight of 1 ct."

This badge from the 26th Triennial Conclave 1895 Knights Templar Boston Chapter was found by Michael K. of Massachusetts with an *AT Pro*. He was searching a large area of untouched woods and hills.

This Confederate saber was found in Virginia with an *AT Pro* by Michael S., in wooded property behind his home.

"I started making my way across a draw and up a small hill to where a trench line is," Michael recalled. "I checked in and around the trenches, finding some relics at about six inches down which my old detector missed. As I moved behind the trenches I got a hit at eight inches deep. I checked the area around the site using the tone to determine how long or wide it is, using the tone as a guide. I figured it measured about thirty inches long. Not knowing what it was, I cleared the debris from the site and started to remove the dirt with a small shovel, a spoon, and my fingers. Within fifteen minutes I uncovered what I thought at first was a piece of band iron and as I removed more dirt, I realized I was looking at a saber/bayonet!"

Through online research, Michael believes his sword may have been an 1856 Enfield bayonet manufactured in London.

Thomas R. was hunting along an old rock wall with his *AT Pro* in New York when he found this 80th Regiment of Foot (Royal Edinburgh Volunteers) buckle. He originally thought the item to be junk metal until he turned it over and saw "REV" written in scrolled letters on the front.

"I was so excited I couldn't speak!" said Thomas. "I couldn't believe what I have found and the rarity of it (two or three known) and why I was digging it up in New York when they were captured in Yorktown, Virginia."

Robert B. from Virginia found this early militia button, dating to the War of 1812 era, with his *AT Max*.

"The *AT Max* proved its worth, sniffing it out amongst the iron by giving that high tone in those irony grunts," said Robert. "The *Max* is definitely a keeper!"

This George Washington inaugural button was found by *AT Pro* user Jason R. of Minnesota. "On a vacation to Massachusetts, I found what I consider to be my best find ever—a George Washington inaugural button from 1789. Research has indicated this button to be one of the more rare varieties of the 26 known varieties. So rare, only ten specimens are known to exist. Auctions have brought anywhere from $1,500-$5,000 for this variety!"

This Union cavalry sword was discovered by John G. of North Carolina with his *AT Pro* while he was searching a stream near a battlefield. The sword remnant was in about a foot of water, with eight inches of mud under it. "The mud preserved it in great condition!" said John. There is even a piece of a leather strap still tied to the scabbard ring."

"You wouldn't believe how many times I thought tin foil was gold!" said Jason B. of Connecticut, an *AT Pro* user. "But there was one day that I rang up a 49-50 on the display. The tone was very solid and I had never seen those numbers before in that succession. In the back of mind I'm thinking, it's gold, it's gold, but the logical part of my brain started kicking in saying, 'It's just another piece of foil or a pop tab.'

"So, I grabbed my trusty trowel and started digging a plug. After I popped the plug out I saw something really shiny. To myself I said, 'Oh, great, another gold colored pop tab.' But as soon as I brought it closer to my face, its shape rounded out and I saw a man's head. I very carefully brushed some dirt away. My heart started pounding. I truly couldn't believe it. After racing home, I further inspected the coin. It was a 12-Mark gold piece from Denmark. The date, 1761, was still legible. It is far from being in good shape, and someone soldered a frame around it, but to me it is my first great discovery, the true diamond in the rough."

This pre-Civil War militia plate (circa 1830-40) was found by Thomas E. from Massachusetts with his *AT Pro* and *Pro-Pointer AT*.

AT Pro user Barbara B. of Alabama *(seen in the lower photo to right)* dug a large gold 1970 class ring from the University of Tennessee. After a few emails back and forth with the university's alumni association, Barbara was able to track down the ring's owner, a local surgeon who had actually done surgery on her arm 25 years earlier! Her story went viral on Facebook and was picked up in overseas newspapers.

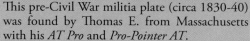

Bryan G. of Tennessee was searching a creek near his home when he got a solid Target ID of 46 on his *AT Pro*. Tucked into the bedrock near a tiny waterfall, he had located a small golden ring, his first ring find.

"My girlfriend staked claim to the little golden ring," said Bryan. "To my amazement, the ring held little red heart garnets, which happen to be her birthstones, set in 14k gold. The ring was a perfect fit as well. This was a Cinderella story to tell about. A year later I'm marrying that girl! I knew Garrett metal detectors were the best detectors in the world, in my opinion, but I didn't know they could find me a wife as well!"

Right: This Scottish Jacobite disc was found near the Georgia state line by Chip K. from Florida, who was searching with an *AT Pro*. Being of Scottish heritage, Chip instantly recognized some of the engravings and slogan on the disc—which he believes came to southeast Georgia in the late 1740s from Scotland.

Chip described some of the engravings and icons on his find: "The disc inscriptions: (obverse) Touch and I Pierce, Aug 23, 1299, W.W., and (reverse) None shall Provoke me with impunity, I make sicker. It is a flat thin silver disc covered with Scottish iconic engravings. There is a lion, thistle, heather, hourglass, a heart pierced by an arrow (means a Jacobite), and a hand wielding a sword stabbing a rose (means Striking at England which is often represented by a rose. This item actually looks like a metal detector)."

Left: David F. of Washington found these 16 gold nuggets with his *ATX* detector while prospecting in Alaska. "From tiny nuggets two inches deep to 3/4-ounce nuggets 14 inches deep, the *ATX* did awesome!" he said.

Kenneth C. of Kentucky dug this 1759 King George II gold 2nd guinea coin on a colonial site on property owned by his grandparents.

Greg M. of Texas shared this story of how he used his *AT Gold* to recover an 1845 $10 gold coin pendant in 2018. "I got a call from a member of our metal detector club THAP, Treasure Hunters Association of Pasadena (TX), who said an asphalt worker named Rowdy from Beaumont lost his 1845 $10 Liberty gold coin pendant while paving a parking lot. I met Rowdy and his crew that next morning at a chemical plant where the parking lot was laid. He and crew had three gold rings between them, so we laid them on the asphalt to get a reading on my *AT Gold*. 76-77.

"The top layer of asphalt is two inches thick, so every target I hit was marked with a quarter. On the third target, we melted and scraped asphalt and found it between the two layers of asphalt. Rowdy, his two crewmen and myself had high-fives and fist bumps happening big time! His mother wore that pedant for years and gave it to him so there was sentimental value. I was really happy and proud to be a part of this. What a great experience!"

William Y. of North Carolina recovered this CSA Atlanta Arsenal style Civil War buckle on private property in Tennessee while using his *AT Pro* and *Pro-Pointer*. After ten years of searching, William felt that he had just found his "Holy Grail of metal detecting."

Above: This horseshoe plaque was made by C. J. Hoag from 1880 to 1890 to commemorate the Grand Army of the Republic, a patriotic group composed of men who had served in the Union forces during the Civil War. Heriberto C. from Connecticut discovered the plaque with his *ACE 350*.

Barry N. from Oklahoma recovered this $5 gold bullion coin necklace with his *AT Pro*. He was hunting a sidewalk area that had been turned up for expansion.

Scott J. of Georgia sent this photo *(above)* of the first seven cannonballs he and his son recovered using their *ACE 250*s. "We found a couple minié balls, then all of a sudden we got a good hit, and dug down and found a 12-pound Civil War cannonball!" said Scott. "We decided to search the area more and when it was all done we found 15 cannonballs total!"

Joe D. of South Carolina found this two-piece Civil War-era Marine buckle with his *AT Pro*. The buckle is shown both before *(above)* and after *(below)* cleaning.

Right: Larry H. of Minnesota found this GAR (Grand Army of the Republic) membership badge that once belonged to a member of this post-Civil War veterans' group. Larry was hunting with an *AT Pro*.

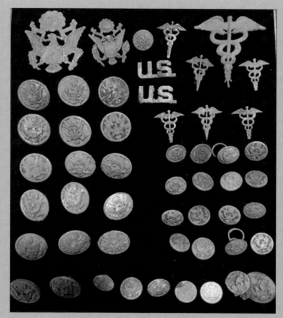

This black powder flask was found by Neil C. of Michigan with his *AT Pro*. Neil's research showed it to have been made in Sheffield, England, around 1860 by the company C&JW Hawsley.

Stone K. of Alabama found an incredible cache of 48 World War I buttons and eleven insignias while using an *AT Pro*.

This 1749 Spanish half reale was found by Nicholas G. of Massachusetts with his *ACE 400*.

Frank M. from California was hunting an old mining camp with his *AT Pro* when he dug his first gold coin— an 1882 $20 piece. Per Frank, the coin sounded as a high tone "right next to the growl of iron."

Erin C. from New York found this War of 1812 artillery button near an old cellar hole in the woods with an *AT Pro*.

Kimmie P. from North Carolina was using an *AT Pro* when she dug a bucket list item—a gold-gilted New York Militia state seal Civil War button. Her research on the discovery site location indicates the button was likely lost in June 1862 by an officer of the 71st New York Militia.

AT Gold user Jeff G. from New York discovered this 1.68-ounce gold nugget in California.

Raymond E. from Texas found this early copper coin with his *AT Pro* while on vacation in the Caribbean. He hired a local guide to help him secure permissions, and was allowed to hunt banana and plantain groves near the site of an old fort that was originally built in the 1400s by Spaniards. Raymond found this "vellon" coin, which had been minted in Saville, Spain, in 1505 by King Ferdinand and Queen Isabella to help stimulate trade in the New World.

This 1881 $10 gold piece was found by John W. from Indiana with his *AT Pro*. New to the detector, he dug a signal that had been a solid 70 on the target ID, fully expecting to find a penny. When he saw his target's gold edge, John expected it to be a token. "But to my surprise, I was holding a gold coin in my hand," he said. "I knew exactly what I was holding the moment the dirt fell off."

This 1787 New Jersey colonial copper coin was found by Eric S. from New Jersey with his *ACE 400*. He was searching a cellar hole that dates to the mid-1700s. *Note: These style New Jersey coppers were actually minted by Eleanor Garrett's great-great-great grandfather, Walter Mould!*

Joe P. from Virginia used his *AT Pro* to recover both the reef and tongue halves of this two-piece Confederate States buckle during the early winter months of 2015.

This 1794 large cent was found by Aggie H. from Ohio with an *AT Pro* at an 1860s home site. She considered it the perfect ending to a long fall day of digging, finding a coin that dated back to George Washington's time in office.

Clarence H. from South Dakota found this gold pocket watch in a local park with his *GTI 1500*. Inside the back cover, he found an 18k marking and a serial number that helped him discover that the watch was made in 1866. Clarence reported that it "took awhile for it to sink in what I had was the best find of my 40 years of detecting."

Don B. from Connecticut was hunting a colonial cellar hole with his *AT Gold* when he found his "dream coin"—a 1787 Fugio one-cent piece. America's first copper penny later became referred to as the Fugio cent after one of the Latin words it contains in its design. This 1787 coin also includes the motto "We Are One," which is surrounded by thirteen chain links that represent the original thirteen colonial states.

"Twenty years of hunting, I have dreamed over finding a Confederate plate," said Lee J. from Virginia. In August 2016, he dug what he considered to be his personal "holy grail." It was a Civil War period Virginia officer's sword belt plate, which Lee said registered as "a solid 88 on my *AT Gold*."

This 1862 $1 gold coin, known as an "Indian Princess" design, was found by Brandon C. from Virginia with his *AT Pro*.

This War of 1812 Light Artillery 1st Regiment flat button was found by Steve V. from Indiana with his *AT Pro*.

"Treasures like this still exist and are waiting to be found," said Steve S. from Massachusetts after finding a silver 1652 Pine Tree Schilling. He was hunting an older site with his son when the coin was recovered. "My son looked at me, and I looked at him and couldn't believe our eyes. I knew it was old but had no idea it was rare. My son and I dusted it off and fell back for a moment, then high-fived each other.

"After being sent to ANACS [American Numismatic Association Certification Service], it was authenticated and graded VF-35 by ANAC," Steve continued. "It's a 1652 NOE 18 Pine Tree Schilling, a find of a lifetime. My son told me this is what keeps him alive in the hobby. You just never know what you are going to dig up!"

Brandon D. from Illinois dug this 14k white gold Eagle Scout ring in a park he was hunting with his *AT Pro*. "After doing some research, it happens to be a Type 1e," said Brandon. "They changed the design in 1937 to a more square art deco design. It breaks my heart to think that a kid worked his butt off to earn such a distinguished honor and lost his ring. I wish there was a name inside so I could return it to him or his family. But I will display it with honor and respect for a time gone by. God Bless America!"

A good mid-range signal led Jamie L. of Oregon to two incredible gold coin finds. "After cutting the plug, I scooped out a handful of dirt to reveal a 1910 Indian Head $5 gold half eagle staring back at me," Jamie said. "I was so excited about the find that I wasn't thinking straight, couldn't focus on detecting any more, and went home to inspect my newfound treasure.

"Laying in bed that night, I realized I had made a critical mistake. I forgot to re-check the hole as I usually do. I wasn't able to get back out for a whole week later, all the while kicking myself for my huge error. When I finally made it back, I immediately went to the same exact spot, turned on the *AT Gold*, and gave it a swing. My heart stopped as I got another distinct mid-range signal.

"I removed the same plug from the week before, and my pinpointer said there was something in it. I carefully tore it apart by hand to discover … a 1906 $5 Liberty! Talk about luck!"

"Second trip out with the *AT Pro* and I almost had a heart attack when I pulled this CSA plate from its prior resting place 10 inches down in south Mississippi," said Travis R. of Louisiana. "There is no way my prior detector would have been able to pick this up."

Left: This .925 silver anchor crucifix was found by James B. of Texas with his *AT Pro*. "Its meaning is hope and security in a storm," he explained.

Left: Sebastian D. from South Carolina found a rare South Carolina Civil War button with his *AT Pro*. This "bushy" palmetto tree version was produced by Eyland and Hayden of Charleston for only a limited period.

Above: This Civil War eagle dog tag was found by Danny C. from Virginia with an *AT Pro*. The soldier, John Vanderpool, was wounded in action in 1862 during the Battle of Gainesville, but lived until 1897.

Service records for this man show him to have enlisted on September 30, 1861, for three years of service. Vanderpool was discharged on October 24, 1864, near Petersburg, Virginia. He was later buried at Green Hills Cemetery, in Dryden, New York.

Mike P. from New York found his first military plate, this 1820–1840 militia buckle, with his *AT Pro*.

Cody M. from Texas dug a 1906 Barber half dollar with a *Treasure ACE 300*.

This inscribed Zippo lighter was found with an *ACE 350* by Brian W. of Ohio. It had once belonged to World War II U.S. Army veteran Jerry Lynn Dyer of the 101st Airborne Division. Dyer was wounded in service for his country during 1967.

Wes and Nick S. used their *AT Gold* and *ACE 250* detectors to find three gold nuggets while on vacation in Colorado.

AT Pro user Larry S. from Iowa dug this 1851 Civil War eagle sword belt plate from soft, moist soil under a tree root in the yard of a 1900s limestone house. Larry's relic recovery is one he considers to be "the best find of my life."

Al W. from Tennessee discovered this tremendous piece of U.S. history with his Garrett *GTA 350*. This oval brass Civil War buckle has the letters "CS," which stand for "Confederate States," and is encircled by 11 stars which represent the eleven Confederate states. It is believed that General Nathan Bedford Forrest had these buckles commissioned for his staff officers.

This 1859-S Seated Liberty dime was found by Steve S. of California with his *GTI 2500*.

Chad T. from Georgia was hunting with his *AT Pro* outside a Civil War camp, where he dug this CSA officer's belt plate. "It was my best find to date," he said.

This 1792 silver Spanish real was dug by Christopher E. from Rhode Island with his *AT Pro* at a colonial house site.

This 1898-S Barber half dollar was found in a vintage silver mesh coin purse that Joe F. from Minnesota recovered with his *ACE 250*. The purse also contained a 1901 V nickel, an 1898 Barber dime, and an 1896 Barber quarter.

Seth E. from Pennsylvania found this U.S. Civil War belt plate with his *AT Pro*. "It was about 8 inches deep and I had to dig through a ton of roots to get it," Seth said. "I just started metal detecting about a year ago. I am 15 now and plan on detecting forever!"

Patrick L. from Massachusetts found this rare Massachusetts Militia officer's sword buckle plate with his *AT Pro*." Finding this buckle was the result of 30% research, 20% intuition, and 50% luck," he explained. Using his kayak, he paddled down a promising-looking riverbank that he had researched during the winter.

He soon had a sharp 70 Digital Target ID signal that showed to be eight inches deep. "It was under a bunch of river bushes and roots and I had nothing but my hands and a small shovel," Patrick said. "The only reason I kept going was the sound in my headset: nice and crisp. Finally got it in my hands. I knew immediately it was a buckle and I recognized the state of Mass emblem, but did not realize what I found until I posted a picture on Treasurenet.com."

AT Gold user Marcus G. dug this Paha Sapa Carnival souvenir in the yard of an 1890s house in South Dakota. The medallion was from the first annual carnival held in 1908 in Deadwood, South Dakota. Marcus was able to take this photo of his relic before turning it over to the landowner.

This 9.9-gram, 18k gold ring is inscribed, "Julia to Mason Xmas 1890" on the inside, and includes a half carat European cut diamond. It was found with an *AT Pro* by Jim K. of Michigan.

Ed H. from Tennessee dug this pair of 1773 Virginia halfpenny coins with his *AT Max*. At the same site in Virginia where he was hunting, Ed found an assortment of round balls and minié balls from the Civil War period.

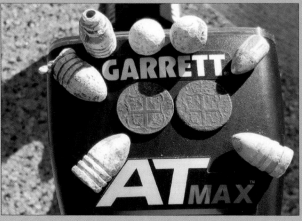

OTHER OUTSTANDING FINDS

Selecting my "Favorite Finds" every month is a great challenge. The preceding section represents only SOME of the past decade's U.S. winners. Trust me when I say that there have been countless thousands of other submissions that were very impressive in their own rights that could have been chosen.

This section includes a small sampling of other customer finds that I've enjoyed over recent years, as well as a few short features on interesting treasure hunts involving Garrett and our customers.

Vaughan Garrett

Left: 1867 two-cent coin, found by *AT Pro* user Randy G. of Kentucky.

Below: Mark S. of Iowa used his *ACE 250* to recover his mother-in-law's lost diamond wedding ring.

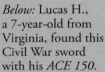

Below: Lucas H., a 7-year-old from Virginia, found this Civil War sword with his *ACE 150*.

14k gold pendant housing a 1997 gold coin, found by James J. of Kentucky with his *ACE 150*.

Platinum diamond ring, appraised at $1,895. Found by Sonny P. of North Carolina with his *AT Pro*.

1856 Seated Liberty dime, found by *AT Gold* user Chase K. of California.

Left: U.S. Civil War artillery grape shot, some seen after electrolysis and some as they appear freshly dug from the ground. These relics were dug by *GTI 2500* user Jimmy K. of Georgia.

An unused Richmond Arsenal cannon fuse *(right)* and a U.S. Civil War-era box plate *(above)* found by John S. of Maryland with his *AT Pro*.

Continental Army uniform button, found by Charlie J. of North Carolina with his *AT Pro*.

Wesley C. of Texas found this sterling silver thimble with his *AT Pro*.

Left: 1902 silver Morgan dollar, found by Leon L. of Louisiana with his *ACE 250*.

1920s Tacoma store token, found by Jared K. of Washington with his *AT Pro*.

Left: World War I general service eagle button, found by Michael L. of Connecticut with his *AT Pro*.

Paul S. of California recovered nearly 70 pieces of gold in two days in a pay patch he located in the El Paso Mountains of Southern California. He was using his *AT Gold* (spelled out in his photo seen above) with a 4.5" *Super Sniper* coil.

"This detector can really sniff out the tiniest flakes of gold!" Paul said. "The smallest piece is a speck at 0.04 grams and the largest of the group is 0.3 grams. I cleaned out the spot of all detectable gold with my *AT Gold*." His two day-haul included more than 6.4 grams of gold. The photo below shows Paul's haul from one of the two days.

Large gold nugget, found by Carole T. of Washington with her *ACE 250*.

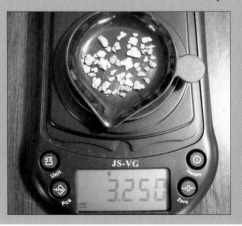

10k gold ring with gem stones, found by Shaun B. of Washington with an *ACE 400*.

Chris V. of Washington took his *Infinium LS* on a two-week Caribbean water-hunting trip and returned with a pile of gold jewelry.

Left: 1852 silver three-cent piece found by Richard M. of Maryland with his *GTI 2500*.

Below: Victorian sterling silver pencil, found by Matt O. of Pennsylvania with an *ACE 350*.

1875 Seated Liberty silver quarter, found by *AT Pro* user Jim G. of Missouri.

Right: 1939 German coin found by Barry S. of Maryland. He was in one of his own pastures, using a *Treasure ACE 100*.

Below: AT Pro user Jeremy C. of New York found this Sea Scouts silver ring.

1851 officer's sword belt plate, found by Robert G. of Texas with his *AT Pro*.

An Indian Head penny tie clip, found by Pedro R. of Texas with his *ACE 250*.

1828 Capped Bust dime, found by Gary J. of Alabama with his *AT Pro*.

14k gold ring with 1.74-carat diamonds, found by Phillip S. of Alabama with his *ACE 250*.

Using his *AT Pro*, Peter D. of New York found this Revolutionary War cannonball 18 inches deep.

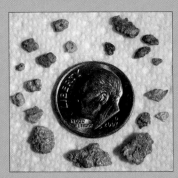

Paul S. and his wife Mary found these 19 tiny gold nuggets in two days of prospecting in California. Using an *AT Gold* with a 4" *Super Sniper* coil, they found nuggets ranging from 0.018 grams up to 0.842 grams.

Left: Jonathan G. of North Carolina used an *ACE 150* to search his old family home, where he found this wedding ring that had belonged to his great grandmother.

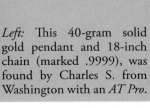

Above: World War II sterling silver U.S. Army medical badge, found by Steven J. of Iowa with an *ACE 350*.

1847 large cent, found by *ACE 350* user Scott S. of Indiana.

Left: This 40-gram solid gold pendant and 18-inch chain (marked .9999), was found by Charles S. from Washington with an *AT Pro*.

1905 W. R. Stoops trade token, found by *ACE 150* user Victor A. of Maryland.

Bill W. of Michigan found this wedding ring ($4,665 appraised) with an *ACE 250*.

18k white and yellow gold diamond necklace with a citrine stone; found by *AT Pro* user Terry S. of Missouri.

1797 Spanish reale, recovered from a lake with a *GTI 2500* by Steve L. of New York.

1849 Seated Liberty dime, with love token design on its reverse. Found by *AT Pro* user Craig K. of Wisconsin.

Small bust pins and two large circular pins depicting Samuel J. Tilden and the year (1876) he ran for president. Found by Perry and Jake E. of Minnesota with their *AT Pro*s.

Right: Lance P. of Illinois decided to buy an *AT Pro* after his wife lost her wedding ring in a small pond. The task of finding it proved to be a challenge, but Lance was up to it. He found the ring, had it professionally cleaned, and decided that he had become hooked on metal detecting in the process of all the searching.

Roy Rogers good luck token, found by Robert M. of Arkansas with an *AT Pro*.

Right: Bob F. of Texas found all these rings and large ear rings during his first 18 months of water hunting with his *AT Pro*.

This large cache of early silver coins was found in a river by Beau O. of Maryland (known on YouTube as "Aquachigger") using an *AT Pro* in 2011. Beau eventually recovered more than 200 coins, dating from the 1780s to 1837.[1]

Massachusetts Volunteer Militia brass belt plate, found by Nick E. of Maine, with his *ACE 250*.

This 1853 Half Eagle 2½ dollar gold coin was found by Jonathan R. of Virginia with an *ACE 350*.

George Washington inaugural button, found by Joshua C. of Maine with an *AT Pro*.

Jim B. of Pennsylvania found this 1825 Capped Bust silver dime using his *ACE 350*.

George "KG" Wyant dug this U.S. Civil War buckle in southwestern Montana while hunting with his *GTI 2500*.

PRESERVING TEXAS HISTORY

Archaeologists and the Garrett search team on the grounds of the San Jacinto battlefield, June 2009.

One of the archaeological projects Charles Garrett and his team participated in during 2009 took place on the most historic battleground of Texas Revolution history.

Once its own independent republic, Texas secured its freedom from Mexico at the Battle of San Jacinto on April 21, 1836. Efforts to preserve artifacts from this conflict have been ongoing, and Garrett employee Steve Moore had worked with archaeologists on site to unearth artifacts on several occasions. The largest effort took place in June 2009, when Charles Garrett and more than a dozen other detectorists joined with the professionals to volunteer at San Jacinto. Within hours that day, many dozens of detected items had been registered by the archaeologists.

Recovered artifacts included dropped musket balls *(above)*, this flat button *(below)*, and this chain from an officer's uniform.

"I feel honored to have taken part in such historic work," said Garrett. "I have always advocated hobbyists to follow a particular code of ethics when it comes to metal detecting. This was a wonderful opportunity for me to practice what I preach and work shoulder-to-shoulder with professional archaeologists and the Texas Parks and Wildlife Department."

Left: Michael Strutt, the Director of Cultural Resources for the Texas Parks and Wildlife Department, thanks Charles Garrett for his team's assistance.

Below: A buckle from a Mexican soldier's shot pouch, found by Charles Garrett.

Right: Garrett holding a musket ball found on the battlefield with his *GTI 2500.*

Note: Garrett metal detectors were used at the San Jacinto Battleground State Historic Site in Texas during controlled archaeological investigations and under the supervision of professional archaeologists. Recreational use of metal detectors is prohibited by law at all Texas State Parks and Wildlife Management Areas.

Anthony R. of Iowa was called upon to find this 3.4-carat diamond ring, insured for $50,000, by an insurance company. Using his *AT Pro*, Anthony was successful.

Water hunters Beau O. of Maryland and Dan F. of Virginia, with some of their *AT Gold* water finds—Civil War rifles and artillery shells (after cleaning).

This spill of Barber coins was found by Mike F. of Wisconsin with his *AT Pro*.

Tiny gold nuggets and a 14k gold ring *(below)* found by Steve H. of Nevada with his *ATX*.

Native American Hoard

Mary T. of Montana went cache hunting in the U.S. Northwest with a couple of friends, hoping to find old silver coins hidden away years ago. She was using her *AT Gold* in All Metal Mode with a large 11" DD searchcoil, when she detected the lid to this copper kettle about 20 inches deep.

Inside, Mary and her friends found it to contain Indian artifacts: many seashells (once used for trade); numerous pieces of chipped obsidian; a hide scraper; strands of beads; a variety of animal bones; several arrow points; ocher rocks used for war paint; and pieces of rolled copper made into "tinklers."

AT Pro user Michael H. of South Carolina found these two diamond rings on the grounds of a middle school built in 1962. They appraised for $9,600 for one and $4,700 for the other.

10k gold 1965 class ring *(see inset)*, found by Ryan H. of Rhode Island using an *ACE 350* in his own back yard.

Aluminum coupon for Ivory soap and a silver 3-cent piece (1851–1873), found by *AT Pro* user Samuel D. of Pennsylvania.

Japanese copper dog tag from World War II, found with an *ACE 250* by Tony F. of Texas.

1723 2-reales coin, minted in Seville, Spain, found by *AT Pro* user James B. of Pennsylvania.

Rodney B. of Ohio dug this 1906 Barber half dollar with his *AT Pro*. Because it was standing on edge, it only presented a Target ID reading of 33.

Mexican two and a half pesos 1945 gold coin, found by Joseph D. of California with an *ATX*.

California / New Mexico saloon token, found by Mike B. of Nevada with an *AT Pro*.

Eric D. found this "Company A" Texas Ranger badge, created from a silver Mexican peso, with his *Sea Hunter Mark II*.

John H. of Texas *(seen above)* has logged countless hours underwater using his Garrett *Sea Hunter Mark II*. He regularly dives rivers and lakes, and enjoys returning lost items to people.

As of 2017, John had found 213 rings *(many seen below)*, plus many watches, phones, and various antiquities. Look to right for more of John's *Sea Hunter* finds: a gold and diamond bracelet; a Cartier watch he recovered for the owner; and an eight-pound cannonball.

Mike L. of Virginia found this 1858 Flying Eagle cent with his *AT Pro* in 2015. It was then his third oldest coin find and the best condition coin he had yet discovered.

Above and below: Jesse W. of Pennsylvania with a Spanish silver 8 reale from 1784, found on the beach with his *AT Pro*.

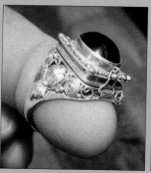 

.925 sterling silver ring, found by Gene S. of Texas, with an *AT Pro* in a Renaissance Festival parking lot.

Lance G. of California found this 1915 California motor vehicle registration tag while hunting with his *GTI 2500*.

Freemason pin, found by *AT Pro* user Randy D. of Missouri.

1652 Pine Tree shilling, found by Michael S. of Maryland with his *AT Pro*.

147 wheat cents, found in a Lucky Strike tobacco tin by Keith M. of California with his *ACE 250*.

GOLDEN PROSPECTS

Buddies Jeff S. *(seen at left in photo)* and Dave F. *(right)* from Washington, made a week-long summer prospecting trip to Nome, Alaska, in 2014.

Jeff, using an *AT Gold*, dug seven pieces of gold (most containing quartz within the nuggets) totaling 1.13 ounces, the largest piece being a third ounce piece.

Dave, hunting with a Garrett *ATX*, netted 2.73 ounces of gold in 16 pieces *(see image below)*. Dave's finds ranged from tiny nuggets only two inches deep to 3/4-ounce nuggets at 14-inch depths.

Left: 1904 World's Fair token, found by Dan L. of New York with his *ACE 350*.

Right: A Grand Army of the Republic Civil War Veterans medal, found by Robert S. of New York with his *ACE 350*.

Left: An 1864–1865 brass United States sword belt plate, found by Chris U. of Colorado with his *AT Gold*.

Left: An 1853 Liberty Head one-dollar gold coin, found by Rich K. of New Jersey with his *AT Pro*.

Right: A 1782 1-reale, found by Sean M. of Delaware with his *AT Pro*.

AT Pro user Curtis M. of Massachusetts found this Revolutionary War period British 74th Regiment button.

AT Pro user Glenn W. of North Carolina found a Civil War camp site that produced more than 220 bullets *(right)* and many other relics, such as the U.S. eagle breast plate and sword belt plate seen above.

This 10k gold Texas A&M class ring was found and returned to its owner by Sean R. of Texas. He made his find with an *AT Pro*.

This Ponds cold cream jar cache of nine V-nickels, dating 1881 to 1905, was donated to the Garrett Museum. It was found in 2013 near an old church by *AT Pro* user Reggie C. of Texas.

Left: 27th New York Infantry Division badge (circa early 1900s), found by Todd B. of New York with his *AT Gold*.

Civil War era frame buckle, found by David S. of Virginia, using a Garrett *Freedom Three CDC*.

Right: Chuck F. of Delaware found this 1780 Maria Theresa Thaler with his *AT Pro*. Originally an Austrian Empire coin, this silver bullion coin continued to be struck for decades as a popular trade coin for the Arabian world.

Gold Spanish coins recovered off Florida with *Sea Hunters* by Scott T. and his dive teams.

Infinium LS searcher Bob S. of Florida found this pair of 4-reale Spanish silver cobs, circa 1619.

1853 Seated Liberty half dime and 1852 silver 3-cent ("trime") piece, found by Evan G. of Oklahoma with his *AT Pro.*

David L. of Washington was able to use his *AT Pro* to help his distraught neighbor find a ring that she had lost while gardening. "I realized my *AT Pro* had paid for itself and then some," said David, "because the look on her face was worth a million dollars."

Soon after moving to Hawaii, Dan P. bought an *AT Pro* to detect in and along the beaches. He found this diamond ring during his first hunt along the water's edge, while using the Pro Mode.

AT Gold user Ryan L. of Utah found these three gold rings in one hole at a soccer field.

1865 two-cent coin, found with *AT Pro* by Ryan G. of New Hampshire.

Left: Rare 1847 Keneta (one cent piece), the first coin Hawaii had commissioned to be minted by King Kamehameha the Third; found by Dan P. of Hawaii with an *AT Pro.*

Right: AT Gold user Freddy F. of Texas found this 1913 Indian Head gold $5 coin.

1830 silver Republic of Mexico 8 reale coin, found by Steve M. of Texas with his *AT Pro*.

Aaron B. of Washington holds one of three coin cache jars he and his daughter found using their *AT Gold*. The cache included two silver half dollars, six Canadian quarters, a buffalo nickel, and 1,038 U.S. clad quarters.

This 1895-O Barber dime—worth well over $1,000—was found by John B. of Kansas with his *ACE 250*.

Don L. of West Virginia was hunting with an *AT Pro* when he found this 14k gold oil derrick ring (with 12 diamonds) and an 18k gold and platinum diamond ring attached to an 18 inch, 14k gold chain.

Civil War Hotchkiss artillery shell, found with an *AT Pro* by Douglas H. of Virginia.

Prospector Steve S. of California found 8.6 grams of gold nuggets while hunting in the El Paso mountain range with his *AT Gold*. The largest nugget seen here weighed 6.7 grams.

Michael C. of Mississippi found this Civil War U.S. baby belt plate with his *AT Pro*.

1938 Radio Orphan Annie (ROA) Secret Society decoder pin, found by Jeff M. of Texas with his *AT Pro*.

Joey D. of Washington found this silver military medallion *(above)* and eleven rings *(below)* with his *AT Gold* in a swimming area.

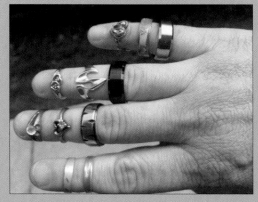

Left: Young Jason B. of Tennessee is all grins over the five Hot Wheels cars he found with his *ACE 250*.

1820 large cent, found by Jeff C. of Connecticut with his *AT Pro*.

Civil War Confederate tongue buckle, found by Shawn K. of Virginia with his *ATX*.

14k wedding band and .925 sterling silver ring, found near a basketball court by John R. of Illinois with his *AT Pro*.

Early 1900s two-horse-vehicle tax badge, found in Florida with an *AT Pro* by Joe E.

1874 Indian Wars buckle, found by Jeffery S. of South Carolina with his *AT Pro*.

Right and inset: Steve M. of Texas with his first gold coin find, an 1851 $1 coin, which he discovered with the *AT Gold*.

An 1806 $5 gold coin, found by Glenn S. of New York while hunting with an *AT Pro*.

Dan from Oregon found this hefty 4.6-ounce gold nugget with his *AT Gold*.

1907 Wabash County Loan & Trust Co. token, found by Steve V. in Indiana with his *AT Pro*.

AT Pro user Brian J. of Pennsylvania found this 1933 Pittsburgh Press marble tournament medal.

1933 Cracker Jack Mystery Club token, found by *ACE 350* user Clem B. of Maine.

1858 Seated Liberty half dollar, found by *AT Pro* user Chris H. of Michigan.

Texas & Pacific Railroad brakeman's hat badge, found by Cody F. of Texas with his *AT Pro*.

Victorian pin, found by Dave S. of Pennsylvania with his *AT Pro*.

Above: Robert W. of California found six silver German coins (dates from 1775 to 1939), made into a bracelet, with the *AT Pro*.

Right: This Civil War Alabama Corps of Cadets button was found by Joseph H. of Alabama with his *AT Pro*.

Right: Gregg P. of Florida found this U.S. Navy watch fob with his *AT Pro*.

This heavy gold nugget ring was found by Steve L. of Texas with an *AT Pro*.

Left: A 1884 Coal Creek Co. 100-script token, found by *AT Pro* user Eric Z. of Tennessee.

Below: A state championship ring found by *AT Pro* user Dan in California.

Cherokee Nation star button *(left and right)*, found by Bruce D. of Oklahoma with an *AT Pro*.

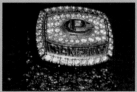

THE "LITTLE DIRT DIGGER"

Emily C. of Georgia goes by the nickname "Little Dirt Digger" on her popular YouTube channel. She is seen here at age 5, with a 1938 Walking Liberty silver half dollar she found with her *ACE 250*.

A 1951 New Jersey Turnpike grand opening token, found by *AT Pro* user Robert D. of New Jersey.

1805 Draped Bust dime, found by Connecticut *AT Gold* user Brandon D.

Early 1900s Freemason ring, found by Justin S. in Oklahoma with his *AT Pro*.

Native American-made silver saddle ring from Albuquerque, New Mexico. It was found by Michael L. from Texas with an *AT Pro*.

Confederate States of America Civil War box plate, found with an *AT Pro* by John T. in Alabama.

Charles F. of Delaware used his *AT Pro* to find a cache of 14 silver coins: seven Franklin half dollars, five Walking Liberty half dollars, and two Peace Dollars.

U.S. Coast Guard class ring, found by Roy L. of Florida with his *AT Pro*.

Silver ring, found by Jon S. of Florida with his *Sea Hunter Mk II*.

AT Pro user Al C. found a 1751 Spanish half reale ring in South Carolina.

METAL DETECTING AND ARCHAEOLOGY

Texas native Ellen J. seen with her *AT Gold* working an Israel archaeology project. Her best find of 2016 was this 135 BC silver shekel *(seen below)*, which features an eagle on the reverse and an imperial profile on the obverse.

Ellen J., a member of the Lone Star Treasure Hunters Club of Dallas, Texas, has spent many of her summers volunteering as a metal detectorist on archaeological projects in Israel. Her first adventure was in May 2013 on the Khirbet el Maqatir dig, where she found herself to be the only experienced detectorist.

"From that two week dig, I was hooked," she said. "I consider it a blessing to combine two hobbies, metal detecting and archaeology, and I've been going back to Israel every summer since."

The detecting began in 2009 when she purchased a *GTI 2500* at the Texas State Fair. Ellen has since added the *ACE 250*, *AT Pro*, and the *AT Gold*. During her first season in Israel in 2013, she found more than 200 coins while helping the archaeology team.

In 2014, she raised her coin total to 300, and added another 250 coins in 2015. Ellen shared, "My goal in 2016 was to cross the 1,000 coin all-time total for Khirbet el Maqatir," said Ellen. "That was done in the first week. The dig director even made a special video of the 1,000th coin. I found 200 more the next two weeks, so we topped 300 for this year and brought the all-time total to over 1,200 coins."

These coins range over many centuries, but the majority are between the 2nd century BC to 1st century AD—making them all about 2,000 years old. Ellen's best coin of 2016 was found using her *AT Gold*, which she uses to go back through dirt piles after sections of soil have been sifted. "I was going over new dirt in the dump when the high tone signal rang loud and clear," she said. "I used the pinpointer to zero in, brushed aside the dirt, and my heart leapt when a large silver coin appeared."

Their Israeli numismatist identified the coin as a Tyrian silver shekel of Antiochus VII, minted in 135 BC in Tyre.

1909 Alaska Yukon Pacific Expo copper medallion, found by Richard B. of Utah with his *GTI 2500*.

Jocelyn Elizabeth, known on her YouTube channel as "Relic Recoverist," found a 1937 Walking Liberty half dollar while testing the Garrett *AT Max* in 2017.

Dylan E. found this Mississippi spur from the Civil War while hunting in Virginia with his *AT Pro*.

Civil War U.S. belt buckle, j-hook, and a minié ball, found by Cody T. of Minneapolis with his *ATX*.

Right: Miguel A. of Texas holds a 95-pound Confederate artillery shell he dug in Virginia with his buddy David H. Found with an *AT Pro*, this Civil War shell is now on display in the Garrett Museum.

INTERNATIONAL FAVORITE FINDS

Vaughan Garrett

When I started the Favorite Finds contest, I simply picked a winner the first few months from all the worldwide entrants. But the volume of submissions from other countries grew so quickly that I decided to select at least one U.S. and one international Favorite Finds winner per month.

This section, once again, is not comprehensive of all of the winners from Vaughan Garrett's Favorite Finds contest. These pages merely represent some of my favorite "Favorites" from the past decade of international winners. Thank you to everyone who has submitted. Keep it up: we might put your picture in our newsletter or select you as a monthly winner!

SOME OF MY **INTERNATIONAL FAVORITES**

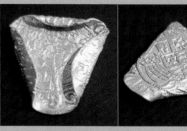

(Above, below) Photos of Michelle's hammered gold coin before and after being professionally restored.

Michelle V. of the United Kingdom was participating in a charity dig, using her *AT Pro International,* when she found her first hammered coin. "I discovered this extremely rare Richard III Half Angel gold hammered coin," she said. "Apparently, it is so amazing that I didn't even realize what I discovered. There are only three known to exist. I found it on a ploughed field about 17 inches down."

Iuliu-Cristenel P. of Europe found this 28-gram ancient Roman gold seal ring using a Garrett *GTI 2500.*

Medieval era bracelet found in Europe by *GTI 1500* user Florian B.

Roman fibula of a two-headed horse, found in Europe by Luka R. with an *ACE 400i*.

Napoleon era British Navy button with beautiful gold plating; found in Europe by Tor H. with his *AT Gold*.

Bronze sealing ring and bronze seal, found with an *AT Pro International* by Adam V. in Europe.

170 pieces of World War II-era German Iron Cross class 2, found by Lucian L. of Europe with his *ACE 300i*.

When Martin B. of the UK attended a rally with his new *ACE 400i*, his best find came just seven paces from his starting point. It was a 40BC Commios "Lawrence" gold stater. "My joy at finding my first gold coin was awesome," said Martin.

Steven E. of the United Kingdom found this 1st Century AD Roman headstud brooch in excellent condition while using his *ACE 400i*. Per Steven, it was a "priceless feeling."

This 35-centimeter (14-inch) Slovenian dagger with decorative wood handle was found in Europe by Tomaz P. with his Garrett *EuroACE*.

Howard M. of the UK found the Bitterley Hoard using his *EuroACE* in 2012. It included one gold James I coin, and 137 silver shillings and half-crown coins, most dating to the 1640s.

Fourteen pieces of Celtic silver jewelry were found in Europe by Gal L. with his Garrett *ACE 350*. The jewelry hoard now resides in a history museum in Romania.

This Australian Imperial Force military return fob, made of 15ct. gold, was given to a soldier after returning home from World War I. It was found with an *AT Pro International* by Danny B. who hoped to track down the family of the soldier to return it.

Cris C. from Canada found this silver 1837/1887 Queen Victoria Jubilee Medal while hunting with an *ACE 250*.

This World War II American soldier's sterling silver ring—with an American seal on front and eagles on each side—was found by Stephen W. from the UK with his *ACE 250*.

NOT JUST YOUR AVERAGE LUCK

Most European searchers would be content with finding a hoard of ancient coins just once in their lifetime. But for Gary S. of the United Kingdom, finding long-forgotten caches is a fairly regular event.

It all began in April 2013, when Gary was searching with his Garrett *EuroACE* metal detector. He dug a Roman radiate bronze coin, followed within minutes by the recovery of four more. He returned to the site the next day, gridded it off, and had dug another 50 Roman coins before he decided it was time to call in the local FLO (Finds Liaison Officer) to report his discovery.

Gary continued to work the site with archaeological experts and after a matter of weeks, the ancient cache total had been run to more than 300 coins. By the summer of 2014, he was using an *AT Pro International* when he found his second Roman hoard, in a field only about ten miles from the site of his first one. This one included 800 Roman bronze radiates that dated to about 260 AD.

Gary's third Roman hoard, about 100 coins, was also found with his *AT Pro*. By December 2014, he had unearthed yet another Roman hoard in a field where he had already made a previous discovery. The Roman bronze coins from this find (made with an *AT Gold*) numbered more than 1,000 and also dated to the 3rd century.

Gary's ability to find such rare treasures is a combination of his diligence in the field, proficiency with the detectors he uses, and the research he puts into seeking new sites. His efforts paid off again in September 2017, when he made another rare recovery while using an *AT Max International*.

During a weekend organized hunt, Gary found a hoard of 14 Bronze Age bun

Upper left: Gary in 2014 with a hoard of coins found while using a Garrett *AT Pro International.*

Above: Close view of hundreds of Roman bronze coins Gary found in 2013 while using a Garrett *EuroACE* detector.

Left: Gary in April 2013 with his hoard of more than 200 bronze Roman coins. During follow-up digs at the site, he would run the total to more than 300 coins found from the ancient cache.

Below: Some of Gary's 3rd century bronze Roman coins, seen as they are unearthed.

Left: Gary dug this Bronze Age goldsmith's anvil, one of only a small number ever found in Europe, in 2015.

Below: This cache of Bronze Age ingots, circa 1000 BC, was found by Gary while using an *AT Max International* in a UK rally during September 2017.

ingots—used around 1000 BC to melt down for forming axes and spears.

With his kind of luck, it is only a matter of time before Gary reports a sixth hoard!

Above: Broken bits of old pottery and hundreds of bronze Roman coins, in a photo taken during the second day of excavating Gary's site in December 2014.

Left: After a mechanical excavator removed a layer of topsoil, Gary continued to scan the area for more coins with his *AT Gold* and *Pro-Pointer*. Several of the Roman coins are seen in the detail inset.

Below: Two of Gary's Roman hoards have been found with parts of the pot that once contained the bronze coins.

Adrian C. *(seen at right)* of Europe found this hoard of Polish and Turkish coins (circa 1599) while hunting with his *ACE 250*. The cache also included an 18k gold ring and an ancient silver ring *(both seen to right)*. Adrian turned over his finds to the national museum of his country.

John W. of Scotland found this 1,500-year-old blue enameled fibula head stud brooch (now on display in the Museum of Scotland) with his *ACE 250*.

Gold nuggets found in Australia by Mark S. with his *ATX*.

A young European searcher named Julian E. using a Garrett *EuroACE* in September 2013 found a hoard of 47,296 silver Ottoman Empire coins, dating 142–144 AD.

GTP 1350 user Jean-Philippe L. of Europe recovered this near-mint condition Byzantine Emperor Justinian II gold coin. Justinian II, the last Byzantine Emperor of the Heraclian dynasty, reigned from 685 to 711 AD.

Gerd M. *(top image)* of Europe dug this Bronze Age bracelet (dating to about 1500 BC) with his *ACE 250*.

This ancient Czech Republic copper axe has been estimated by archaeologists to be between 4,200 and 6,500 years old. It was found by Roman C. of Europe while he was using a Garrett *EuroACE*.

European Rafael T. recovered a 16th Century Medieval hoard while using his *AT Pro International* and *Pro-Pointer*. "Hunting over two fields where we got permission, I found 14 Medieval silver coins," he said. "Eight beautiful coins were in the same hole and the others not so far. I believe it was a Medieval hoard scattered by years of plowing."

Lecat R. of Europe found this gold Louis the Pious (778 to 840 AD) coin with his *EuroACE* detector.

Lecat, who detects on the weekends and digs everything, said this coin recovery was a "big surprise." He estimates it to be 8th century, and said the middle cross symbolizes Christ, while the four small dots represent the four Gospels proclaimed to the four corners of the earth, beginning in Jerusalem.

This 8th Century Celtic annular brooch was discovered by Seán M. from the UK with his *AT Pro*. Per Seán, it is gold gilded, with red glass beads to represent the eyes of a beast.

A Celtiberian plate, circa 500 BC, found by Julen R. with an *ACE 250* in Europe. The Celtiberian people were of Celtic origin and lived in Spain before the Romans.

This late Medieval silver signet ring was discovered by Suzie F. of Europe with a *EuroACE*.

Right: During a Dutch rally, Wilfred H. found this 1755 gold ducat coin with his *AT Pro International*. He at first assumed the Target ID signal of 62 would be a piece of lead.

Above: 1837-1897 Queen Victoria 60th Jubilee Commemorative medal, found in Australia with an *ACE 250* by Mike S.

Edward the VI silver shilling (circa 1551-1553), found with an *ACE 250* in the UK by Simon B.

Krystyna Z. of Europe lost her confirmation ring the day she got it in 1951. After years of thinking that metal detecting was dangerous and reserved only for the military, Krystyna picked up an *AT Pro* to search the area where she lost her ring. After scouring the beach, she decided to search the shallow water and she found her own long-lost ring.

Right: ACE 250 user Bart H. of Europe found this gold florin, dated around 1315.

Left: Celtic gold stater coin, found by John B. in the UK with a *EuroACE*.

Right: 1920s gold and diamond art deco ring, found by Rein S. in Europe with a *EuroACE*.

3,000-YEAR-OLD GOLD TREASURE

These photos show the ancient gold chain links found by *AT Pro* user Fanel S. in the recovery hole *(above)* and after cleaning.

Fanel S. of Romania, a pastor by trade, often reserves his Mondays for his favorite hobby of metal detecting with his *AT Pro*. In early 2014, he made a recovery on an old school grounds that was deemed exceptional by the National History Museum of Romania.

Along a steep slope, his *AT Pro* gave a nonferrous metal indication, which he assumed would be another World War II brass cartridge, a common find in his area.

"I started to dig, hoping whole-heartedly not to find again a cartridge case," he said. "At 20 to 30cm depth, I saw a part of the first link. This cut my breath. I recognized instantly what it was because only one month ago, about 1 km away, I discovered four golden rings of the same kind. After my explosion of joy and excitement ended, I worked very carefully to take the rings out of the ground. My surprise was great when I saw it was not just a link or two, but it was a handful of chain links—21."

Fanel followed his country's laws by handing over the golden links to the National History Museum of Romania. Their specialists used X-ray identification to determine that the chains were 86% gold and 14% silver. Fanel

said the local alluvial gold weighs 115.57 grams and was considered to be "an exceptional discovery in Romania. Archaeologists dated the chain links around the 12th Century BC, meaning they are about 3,000 years old."

Viking fibula, circa 1050 AD, found by Ole B. with an *AT Pro International*.

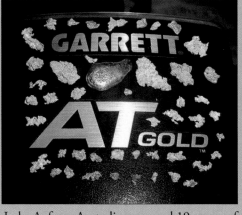

Luke A. from Australia recovered 19 grams of gold with his *AT Gold*.

ROMAN AND VIKING HOARDS: THE GARRETT LADS

(Above and below) Obverse and reverse views of 20 and one third of the silver Roman denari coins found by Daniel and Justin on the hoard site.

Daniel and Justin pose with their Roman coin hoard in 2013.

Justin B. of the United Kingdom received a Garrett *EuroACE* for his birthday in February 2013, and soon became friends with Daniel B., who acquired an *ACE 250* that spring. The two quickly became regular hunting partners, referring to themselves as the "Garrett lads."

During their first full summer of searching, the lads had the good fortune of discovering a hoard of more than 20 Roman silver coins. They each found one silver coin during the first evening in July, but returned the next day to dig another 19 Roman coins from an area of about ten square meters. Their local Finds Liaison Officer (FLO) named the find the "Lowside Quarter Hoard" after the parish where their find was made.

The following summer, in 2014, the Garrett lads found another silver hoard, this one dating to 10th century Viking history. It was the hiding place of almost 1kg of Viking silver—16 solid silver ingots and four rings. Daniel found the first ingot, only two inches in length, with his *EuroACE*. Justin, searching with an *AT Pro* about a foot away while inspecting Daniel's find, then recovered a silver ingot almost four inches in length and one inch wide, weighing 128g. It is one of the largest to be found in the UK.

Justin and Daniel's hoard was properly reported to local archaeologists with the British Museum. "It was a magical find," according to Justin.

"Garrett lads" Daniel and Justin found their second hoard during the summer of 2014, using an *AT Pro* and a *EuroACE*. The silver ingots and jewelry pieces were examined by archaeologists, who declared the find to be a significant Viking hoard dating to about the 990 AD period.

Gold Pendant from the Viking Age, found by Martin N. in Europe with his *AT Pro*.

Carl G. from the UK was searching a very small field with his *ACE 150* in the rain when he dug his first gold coin, a George III gold guinea from 1775.

This silver Slovak Armed Forces Badge of Honor, instituted in 1942, was awarded to men who had served in combat on the Russian front during Hitler's 1941 invasion of Russia. It was found in Europe by Lubos with an *AT Pro*.

Peter G. of South Africa was searching with his *ACE 250* on an 1890s battle site between the Boers and British Army when he found this heart-shaped silver matchbox, apparently lost by one of the British soldiers.

Dragos S. of Europe was one of my Favorite Find winners with this 12th Century bronze-cast reliquary cross, discovered with his *AT Pro International*. He donated his find to a local museum to put on display.

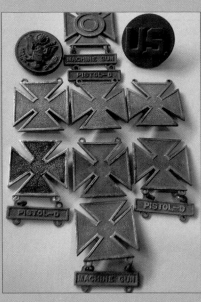

Right: John S. of Australia used his *AT Gold* to search the remnants of a World War II military camp once occupied by the U.S. Army. He detected a rubbish pit that was filled with silver rifleman's medallions.

"I began to shake, and got quite emotional as one after the other continued to appear . . . eight in all!" John said.

Right: Juan C. from Chile found this military sword with his *AT Pro* near the scene of the 1873 Battle of Palo Seco.

A golden Medieval crown cufflink, found by *EuroACE* user Tamas H. of Europe.

Rare 40 AD Celtic Gold Stater, discovered by Jason M. from the UK with his *AT Pro International*. "The coin came out of the ground in perfect condition," he said.

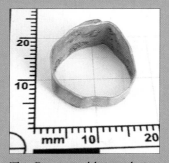

This Roman gold ring, dating to the period of 150 to 300 AD, was found by Maik in Germany with an *AT Pro International*.

This 14th Century cross was discovered by Bjørnar H. of Europe with his *AT Pro*. "It is made of a metal called Electrum," he said, "which is a naturally occurring alloy of gold and silver, with trace amounts of copper."

Mark E. from Bermuda discovered this 14k gold pocket watch *(seen after cleaning)* with his *Sea Hunter Mk II* in the waters off the beach.

"I was out with my Garrett *AT Gold*, detecting a plowed field," said Dennis M. of Europe. "I got a really fine signal (actually the first signal of the day), and it turned out to be a fragment of a bronze sword that dates back to between 1,000 and 1,500 BC. I began to search the surrounding area and three meters from the first piece, the second piece emerged. And then another, and another. In the following hour, a total of eight pieces came out of the ground, revealing a complete Bronze Age sword! It measures 48 centimeters and weighs 348 grams. I brought it to the museum, and they were thrilled to say the least! Best day of detecting ever!"

This Antoninus Pius silver denarius Roman coin (circa 138 AD) was found by Keith W. from the United Kingdom. He was hunting an eight-acre site, where he used his *AT Pro International* to find other Roman coins.

Virvarei C. and his friend Valeriu from Europe found a cache of 161 silver 18th and 19th Century Ottoman coins in 2014. Virvarei and his friend were hunting a place that was the heart of a village burned to the ground during the war. The area they were searching had tall grass and thorns, and in one particular square meter it was really dirty, with many targets. Virvarei was using an *ACE 250*, and his friend used an analog VLF machine.

Virvarei described their discovery. "My friend got a strong signal and said it was too strong, probably just big iron. I said 'May I try? Let me see what my machine says.' I passed the coil over it and immediately the last cursor of the display clearly indicated silver! If it were large iron, the cursor oscillates left and right, but here it stayed stuck there from the beginning. I said, 'Let's dig!'

"We started to dig four inches, 10 inches, and suddenly at 13 inches we found a piece of pottery…a broken one, looking really bad. We pinpointed again the target, no change, strong signal. After a few handfuls of soil, we saw the rest of the pot, painted green, no doubt medieval, and for sure containing something. Val slowly lifted the bowl from the pit and said, 'Man, it's heavy, at least 5 kilos!' Adrenaline exceeded by far the maximum level!

"Suddenly we saw the silver surface of a very large coin, about 5 cm in diameter and with Arabic lettering. The bowl was full! After 10 minutes of assumptions, congratulations, handshakes, and happy faces, we found that the bowl contained 161 silver Ottoman coins,

minted in Constantinople in the eighteenth and nineteenth centuries. Each coin weighs 27 grams. It was a dream. A dream possible because of my adventure companion, my *ACE 250*, bought four years before, and as you see, still reliable."

Cache of seven bronze and silver Roman coins found in the same hole by fourteen-year-old Sean P. from Europe with his *EuroACE*. He stated enthusiastically, "This was one of the best experiences of my life!"

2,000 year-old silver Roman fibula, found by Rune I. of Europe with his *ACE 250*.

Stefan D. of Europe recovered this large gold coin with a *GTI 2500*, while searching a forest where he had found other Roman coins. It is an 8.98-gram 1st Century Roman Aureus double solidus coin.

Joshua C. of Canada recovered a sterling silver World War II Royal Canadian Air Force memorial bar while hunting with his *AT Pro*. These silver bars were presented upon death to the families of fallen soldiers. The flight officer honored in this plaque died in service to his country on December 2, 1943. Joshua intends to try to return the lost item to the family.

This hoard of 128 silver hammered coins was discovered by Savvas C. from the UK with his *EuroACE* and *Pro-Pointer*. Savvas described them all as Tudor groat and half-groat coins from the reign of Henry VII (1485-1509), father of Henry VIII.

This cache of five Roman gold coins was found by Davorin K. of Europe with his *ACE 250*.

ACE 150 user Rafal S. of Europe found a pair of World War II Special Forces Zeiss Wehrmacht binoculars.

This collection of four golden roubles was found by Yurii K. of Europe and his friend with the *GTI 2500*.

"I dreamed about golden coins," said Yurii. Over the course of four days, the two searched near an old foundation, where Yurii dug his first two coins: a 1900 5-rouble and an 1899 10-roubles.

Dale M. of New Zealand submitted this photo of 101 gold rings he had discovered with his Garrett *ATX* in 2014 on the beaches and in the ocean water. They range from 9ct to 24ct gold. Dale reported that he often used the 8" mono searchcoil for water hunting.

This early gold coin, known as a Pseudo-Imperial Tremissis (circa 550 AD), was found by Mark V. from Europe with an *ACE 250*.

This rare Celtic gold quarter stater (circa 50 BC) was discovered by Chris B. of the UK with his *ACE 250*.

David M. of the UK found this Bronze Age gold clothes fastener with his *ACE 150*. Experts have estimated it to from about 1200 BC.

Gold ring money was used as currency by ancient Celtic tribes. This piece, dating to the Bronze Age, was discovered by Pete H. from the UK with his *ACE 250*.

A silver denarius-Commodus Roman coin, discovered by Frentescu L. from Europe with his *EuroACE*.

Duane R. from Canada found this pair of Jesuit rings (dating to the late 1600s) three feet from each other with his *AT Pro*.

Two gold Medieval rings, discovered by Michal P. from the UK with his *AT Pro*. They date to about 1400–1550 AD.

South Ferriby gold Celtic stater (45–150 BC), found by Russell M. from the UK with his *AT Pro*.

Dan K. of Canada dug this 1795 Flowing Hair silver dollar (3 leaves version) with his *AT Pro* and *Pro-Pointer AT*. "At the time, I had no idea what I had other than a monster silver coin," said Dan.

A half-ounce gold nugget, discovered by David K. from Australia with his *ATX* with a 10 x 12 DD coil.

This Byzantine brass ring was found near an old village site by Nikolay P. with his *EuroACE*.

Medieval silver ring with red stone, discovered by Luka H. from Europe with his *ACE 400i*.

A rare Aureus of Severus Alexander gold coin, found by Bruce H. from the UK with his *AT Pro International*.

These five golden Roman coins were found in Europe by Miralem B. with his *AT Pro International*.

The first coin was of Emperor Gratian (367–383 AD) and the other four he found were Emperor Valentinian the Great (364–375) coins.

Rains had made his search area very muddy. "I was dirty as a pig but in one hour I had found five golden Romans!" said Miralem.

Set of Royal New Brunswick Regiment buttons, found by Brock P. of Canada, with his *AT Pro International*. This regiment existed from the late 1700s to 1803.

This military buckle with the image of a lion belonged to an officer of the Paraguay Army in the 1860s. It was found by Ezequiel R. from Argentina with his *ACE 350*.

These six gold nuggets, the largest weighing nearly 1.5 ounces, were found with an *ATX* by Glen B. from Australia.

This 17th century gold fede ring, consisting of twisted loops and clasped hands, was found by Wilfred de H. in Europe with his *AT Pro International*.

Adam C. from the UK found this U.S. Army soldier's dog tag with his *EuroACE*. Adam then began researching the man, who had passed away in 1995. He was able to reach Private Anthony's surviving niece, who was overjoyed to have her uncle's World War II dog tag returned from overseas. "God bless your heart," she told Adam.

Martin F. from the UK shared this exciting story of a 518-coin Roman hoard, located with his *ACE 250*.

"Whilst searching a new field on July 25th, 2013, with my trusty nine-year-old *ACE 250* with double D coil, I had been searching for over an hour with my friend Jeremy when I got a deep signal but good. I started digging and after 14 inches, there was nothing but the great signal. I called Jeremy over as he had a pinpoint probe and mine was broken. We scanned the hole and carried on digging. We hit a stone and on pulling it out we found four Roman coins stuck to it! I shouted, "Stop!'

"Upon examination, we found coins loose and stuck in the soil, all bronze and in good condition. We knew it was a hoard, but how big? We stopped and contacted the museum finds officer and the land owner who both came out very excited. It was agreed to excavate the hoard in three days time, so we had to bury the find again and maintain complete secrecy to protect the site. We came back three days later with the finds officer and did a complete 8-hour excavation, documenting the dig in photos, drawings and video."

Martin said the cache weighed about 2.5 kilograms (5.5 pounds) and was buried in a bag. The British Museum discovered that all the coins were from the period 260–295 AD of various Gallic and Britannic emperors. "The coins were buried in three separate Hessian bags stuffed with leaves to keep the coins from clinking, then buried in a leather bag," said Martin. "The leather and leaves were still intact in places! The coins were declared treasure and were valued at £1619."

Raja K. of Malaysia found this Arabic gold coin with his *AT Gold*.

Bjorn S. and four of his friends—Heinrich O., Lars H., and Simon K.—shared a terrific recovery with their *AT Pro*'s. An elderly lady told one of the four European men a centuries-old legend that there would be a silver treasure in a certain area of a field outside Herning. The legend proved to be true, as the four men detected and found 50 silver coins from the period of Danish Monarch Christian IV (1586-1656).

This 16.3 gram electrum gold stater, from the period of 500-460 BC, was discovered by Taras S. from Europe with his *AT Pro International*.

James M. from the UK found this Medieval silver Klippe coin, an 8 ore from 1564, with his *AT Pro International*. This coin was stamped during the Nordic Seven Years' War and was a way of quickly paying the soldiers.

These Bronze Age silver and gold nose rings were found by Fanel S. with his *AT Pro International*.

"These two rings were analyzed by archaeologists and dated as belonging to the Early Bronze Age specific objects—3500 years BC," he said. The 27mm gold ring weighs 15 grams, while the slightly larger silver ring weighs in at only eleven grams.

This six deniers 1711 coin was found by Mario L. from Canada with his *AT Pro International*.

This 13.2 gram gold Birka crucifix was found in Denmark with a *EuroACE* by Dennis H. This 10th century cross, called the "Aunslev Cross," provides evidence that Christianity was adopted in Denmark earlier than what had previously been accepted.

"Until now, the Jelling Stone has been the oldest Christian evidence in Denmark, but my crucifix has now amended that," said Dennis at the time. "My discovery has aroused enthusiasm among amateur and full-time archaeologists. People from all over the world have contacted me on Messenger and congratulated me on the item."

A hoard of seven gold French coins, found in Europe by Harreau L. with his *ACE 250*.

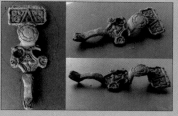

Iron Age fibula and ring brooch, found by Rune N. from Europe with his *AT Pro International*.

John K. of the UK found a hoard of Roman coins with his *AT Pro International*. A landscape gardener, John was given permission to scan the soil excavated from a client's property who was digging a 6-foot-deep coy carp pond.

John found six Roman silver coins, the oldest dating to the reign of Mark Anthony (32–31 BC). He also found one gold coin *(seen above)*, one including the mark of Emperor Vitellius, who ruled in 69 AD.

About a month after buying his *AT Gold*, Anghel T. of Europe made a tremendous discovery. He found a silver Roman denarius coin and called to his friend, who was using an *AT Pro*, to join him. "We searched the area," Anghel said. "After ten seconds, beep, beep. Signal 80 to 81 on the display; small hole, new coin! Okay, let's split, *AT Pro* on one side, *AT Gold* the other side. Lots of signals, lots of holes, and YES, lots of coins."

By the end of the day, Anghel and his friend had recovered 242 total silver Roman denarius coins (circa 90–41 BC), which were turned in to their country's national museum.

18th Century sword guard, found by Vania R. of Europe with his *ACE 250*.

Dan S. from Western Australia found these 15 ounces of gold with his Garrett *ATX*. "Incredible machine in highly mineralized ground," Dan said. His largest nugget weighed in at 6.5 ounces.

Steve B. from Canada found this 18 gram, 18k gold ring at an old school with his *AT Pro International*. He dug this monster Aztec ring close to the metal goal post of a soccer net. "I took a picture of the ring in the plug, wiped it off, and threw it in my pouch, thinking it was a junker ring," Steve related. "After the 8-hour hunt, I cleaned off the ring and saw that it was reddish color and had a stamp on the back marked 18k.

"I gave it a salt and vinegar bath which removed the reddish color, then gave it a baking soda and water paste rub to clean it up more. This is when I noticed the color changed to yellow goldfish tone." Steve received mixed opinions on his "gold" ring after posting it online, so he took it to a jeweler to have it acid-tested.

"Sure enough, it tested positive for 18k gold!" he said. "I was shocked he offered me $500 cash for the ring on the spot, but I refused to sell it but instead paid $20 to get it polished up. I later looked up the melt value, and based on the weight of the ring at 17.4 grams, it's worth between $700-750 CDN. This is such a weird but amazing find due to the discoloration of the ring coming out of the ground, which must have been there for 50-60 years to tarnish this way. 18k is 75% gold mixed with 25% copper, so I'm guessing that's why it had that color to it."

This Visigothic gold coin, from the reign of King Recesvinto in 649 to 672 AD, is known as a tremis (meaning "a third of a unit"). It was found in Europe by Antonio P. with his *AT Pro International*. He was searching a recently plowed section of forest land at the time.

Nicola P. of Europe dug this collection of German military artifacts using an *ACE 250*. They include two Iron Crosses, a War Merit Cross, a wound badge, and a land combat badge for the German Luftwaffe aviation unit.

Potapov E. of Russia dug 4,500 kilograms of silver treasure using his *ACE 250*, which he calls his "workhorse." His massive haul of silver included 36 bars of solid silver and 160 silver coins from more than a half dozen khan who ruled in the 1300s and 1200s.

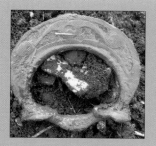

Paula P. of the UK found this crescentic terret ring from an Iron Age chariot (circa 100 BC) with her *AT Pro International.*

ACE 400i user Tomislav B. of Europe found this gold Roman coin.

Gold Roman denarius from Emperor Antemio (453 AD), found by in Europe by Germano F. with his *ACE 250.*

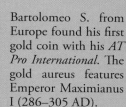

Bartolomeo S. from Europe found his first gold coin with his *AT Pro International.* The gold aureus features Emperor Maximianus I (286–305 AD).

This 18 karat gold and diamond ring was found on a beach by Martyn P. of South Africa with his *AT Pro International.*

A German officer's World War II ring, found by Guta D. of Europe with an *ACE 250.* Its inside is engraved with "Warschau 1941."

Harry M. of the UK decided to spend an hour in the field after work with his *AT Pro International* and was rewarded with a tone reading in the high 70s. "I dug, and out popped a gold disk covered in mud," said Harry. "My first thought was the dreaded bottle top or something similar but when I picked it up, it had some weight to it. I saw through the mud lettering and I immediately dropped it and freaked out. I pulled out my phone to film for my YouTube channel and so I wiped the mud off, and in front of me was the most beautiful mint condition gold Roman coin."

A British Navy officer's button from the Napoleon War era, found by Tor H. from Europe with his *AT Gold.*

Hamza A. from the UK found this Merovingian Frankis gold tremissis coin (circa 585–675 AD) with his *AT Gold,* while hunting a very trashy field in a club hunt.

OTHER DESERVING FINDS

Vaughan Garrett

Selecting my "Favorite Finds" every month is a great challenge. The preceding section represents only SOME of the past decade's winners. There are so many thousands of other brilliant finds submitted each month that I figure it is worth a few more pages here to show just some of them. Even though these treasure finds were not selected in my monthly Favorite Finds contest, I still consider each and every one to be impressive.

Thanks again to all our many Garrett customers who have taken the time to thoughtfully submit their stories and photos!

Right: Hammered silver coin found in the UK with a *EuroACE* by Morley H.

Left: Jean-Philippe L. of Europe found this Roman gold ring, engraved with a palm tree branch, with a *GTAx 1250*.

Left: 1779 George III gold half guinea, found by Andrew C. of the UK with his *AT Pro International*.

Right: A torque necklace with mother of pearl or oyster shell inlays; found by Clark S. of the UK with his *AT Pro International*.

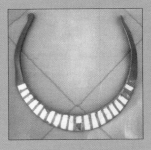

Left: Three coins found by Julian G. of the UK with his *ACE 250*. Left to right are a 1918 silver sixpence, an 1859 gold half sovereign, and an 1898 silver half crown.

Left: Australian 103rd field battery artillery badge, found by Aussie *AT Pro International* user Craig A.

Right: Roman Sesteritius coin, found in Europe by *EuroACE* user Rok H.

Third Reich German policeman hat badge, found in Europe by *EuroACE* user Michal D.

1827-B Willem I gold 5 gulden coin, found by Jaap S. of Europe with his *AT Pro International*.

Julia Lepedia Roman bronze coin (ca. 44-36BC), found with a *GTI 2500* by Adrian R. of Europe.

Kevin M. of the UK was detecting in a club charity event in November 2017 with his *AT Pro International* when he discovered this hoard. Dating to the late 2nd Century or early 3rd Century, this cache contained more than 200 Roman Antoniniani coins.

Right: Mark Anthony silver denarius coin, circa 31-32 BC, found in the UK by Gordon W. with an *ACE 400i*.

Left: James I gold quarter noble coin, found by Martin F. of the UK with his *ACE 250*.

Silver coin cache, circa 1587-1668, found by Piotr W. of Europe with an *AT Pro International*.

Two 3rd Century BC Celtic silver coins *(obverse and reverse of each seen to left and right)*, found in Europe by Simon R. with his *AT Pro International*.

THE GTI 1500 ROMAN COIN HOARD

Ian B. of the United Kingdom dug this cache of more than 2,800 4th Century bronze Roman coins in November 2007. He was detecting a plowed field in Shropshire County, England, with his *GTI 1500* when he found his first scattered coins, along with a bronze ring.

After contacting his local Finds Liaison Officer to properly report his treasure, Ian returned to the field and finally located large quantities of the bronze coins. In addition, he unearthed a large, crumbling pot that had once housed the hoard. The final coin count was 2,855.

Left: Paulo S. of Europe found this ancient gold coin with his *EuroACE* detector. It is from the period of Emperor Honorius (394–423 AD).

German Labor Day medallion from 1943, found by Air Force veteran Thomas T. with his *AT Pro*, while he was stationed in Europe.

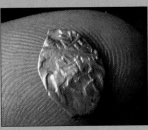

Mikhail Fedorovich silver coin from the 1600s, found by *AT Pro International* searcher Aleksandr B. in Europe. Seen on the tip of his finger, these tiny silver coins are nicknamed "fishscales."

Above: 1664 Austrian 15-Kreuzer silver coin, found by Adam V. with an *AT Pro International.*

Right: Religious pendant found in Thailand by *Sea Hunter* user Brent M.

9k gold lion's head ring, found with *ACE 250* by Andrew L. of the UK.

Right: Bulgari 18k gold ring with 24 diamonds, appraised at $3,650. Found by John H. of the UK with his *Sea Hunter Mk II.*

Polish Zikmund III silver coin minted in 1536, found in Europe with an *ACE 250* by Jan M.

"I am so glad I got into this sport," said Petr K. *(seen below with one of her brass relic finds)* of Europe. In her first two years using an *ACE 250*, she found many old silver coins *(see photo at left)* and "some cool and old artifacts."

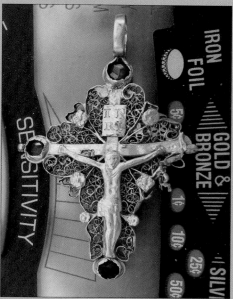

This 18th century yellow gold cross, believed to be an ornament worn by the wealthy, was found with an *ACE 250* by Felix M., in a European plowed field.

Aurélien B. of Europe found his first gold coin using the Garrett *EuroACE* detector. His gold florin coin, dating to 1362–1370 AD, depicts John the Baptist on one side.

One gold and two silver Roman coins found in Europe by a *GTP 1350* user. The rare gold coin was valued at about €20,000.

While on vacation in Central America, Don N. of Indiana used his *AT Pro* to find these three Carolus silver reals and six Spanish cobs from the 1700s.

Barry C. of Canada found this inscribed silver Memorial Cross with his *GTI 2500*, and returned the World War II medal to the soldier's family.

Above: Shigeki K. of Japan found this 50 sen coin, dated 1922, with an *ACE 250*.

Below: Two more of Shigeki's finds—an 1873 1 sen copper dragon coin and *(lower)* an early 1700s 40-mon coin.

Left: World War I Army cap badge, found in the UK by *AT Pro International* user Rob J.

Below: Scott H. of the UK used his *AT Pro International* to find a hoard of Roman denarius coins in 2012. In all, Scott dug 211 complete and 69 partial coins, estimated to be about 2,000 years old.

1674 Charles II farthing, found by *ACE 250* user Dave B. of New Zealand.

Left: Celtic quarter stater, circa 70 BC featuring a triple-tailed horse, found with a *GTI 1500* by Dave W. of the UK.

Hoard of Russian silver coins, found in Europe by Alexander L. with an *ACE 250*.

Polish 1615 silver Sigismund III coin, found with a *EuroACE* by Nazar D. of Europe.

This hoard of 6,000 Roman bronze coins from the 3rd Century, found buried in this large pot, was discovered with a Garrett *GTAx 550* by Ron H. of the UK.

Above: Roman artifacts found in Europe by Dalibor B., using an *ACE 250*.

Ovidiu P. of Europe *(above)* found this hoard of more than 75 silver Roman coins—dating between 350 to 384 AD—with his *GTI 2500*.

Left: Brass World War I belt clips, with Russian style at top and Austro-Hungarian version below. They were found with a *GTI 2500* by Boris D.

Right: This diamond cross chain was found by John W. of Canada with his *AT Pro International.*

A cap badge from World War II resistance fighters, found with an *ACE 250* by Grega J.

Burdy A. of Europe found two silver rings and 22 silver Medieval coins along a stone path with a Garrett *EuroACE.*

Below: A 1720s gold coin, found by Luis S. of Europe with a Garrett *EuroACE.*

Right: Øystein M. of Europe found this bronze horse from the Viking Age using an *AT Pro.*

Roman Cassi silver denarius, found in Europe with an *AT Pro International* by Benjamin K.

Left: An 1873 Victorian gold sovereign coin, found by Michael J. of the UK with his *ACE 400i.*

7th century silver Anglo Saxon sword pommel cap, found by James E. of the UK with his *ACE 400i.*

18k gold ring, found in Canada by Randy K. with an *Infinium LS.*

BYZANTINE GOLD COIN HOARD

Peter W. *(seen at left, above)* and his friend Niels pose with 47 gold Byzantine coins they recovered with their Garrett *AT Pro International* detectors. Most of the coins (ca. 465–585 AD) were in excellent condition.

Peter said that he was hunting an old farm that he had been led to by his research. He and Niels had spent considerable time creating their own map depicting all the known gold, silver and bronze coins found in their region during the past 200 years. "We found a pattern of gold coin findings in the region we have been searching," Peter explained. "In that pattern, there was an un-filled area, so I decided to go on and search this area." He was more than two hours into his search of the farm when he dug his first gold coin. "At first I thought it wasn't real and put the coin in my bag," he said.

"Then at the same spot, I got the same pitch; this went on and on." Peter quickly called his friend to come join him with his *AT Pro*. When Niels arrived an hour later, Peter had already dug 32 gold coins. "After four days of searching, we found a total of 47 coins," said Peter, who recovered 40 of them.

He believes the ancient cache was once contained in a pot or sack that was hit by a tractor plow. The coins were found in an area only about 15 meters in length and at depths ranging from about 10 to 35 cm (4 to 14") deep. The coins were properly documented by European authorities and returned to Peter and Niels. If the cache is eventually sold for profit, the landowner will share in the proceeds, according to local law.

Roman silver coin depicting Emperor Titus, ca. 79 AD. Found by *AT Pro International* user Alexander C. in Europe.

1725 Peter the Great 1-Ruble silver coin, found by Teemu V. of Europe with an *ACE 250*.

Confirmed by UK finds liaison officer to be a Bronze Age socketed spearhead (circa 1600–1300 BC), this artifact was recovered by Marc P. of the United Kingdom with an *ACE 250*.

Second century Roman silver signet ring, found in Europe by *ACE 250* user Segiu C.

Olinskí G. of Europe found this decorative dagger on the stony bottom of a mountain stream, at the site of a principal crossing point used on the river since the 1640s. He was using his *AT Pro*.

Four British military breastplate martingales (circa 1840-1850), found in Canada by David K. with his *ACE 350*.

This historic ring *(seen above and below)* was found with an *AT Gold* by Dennis M. of Europe. He was hunting off an island where a castle had been torn down in 1677 when he recovered this gold and diamond ring. Museum officials in Denmark believe the ring may have been a gift from King Christian the 4th to his second wife.

This hoard of 220 ancient Greek silver coins, dating to the 2nd century BC, was found in Europe by Fanel S. with his *AT Pro International*. Fanel is seen below with one of his sons as he recovers the coins from a hillside.

WWII sterling silver Combat Infantryman Badge (CIB), found in Europe by Nicola P. with an *ACE 250*.